# THE POETRY OF SAPPHO

# THE POETRY OF
# SAPPHO

Translation and Notes by

## JIM POWELL

OXFORD
UNIVERSITY PRESS

2007

# OXFORD

UNIVERSITY PRESS

Oxford University Press, Inc., publishes works that further
Oxford University's objective of excellence
in research, scholarship, and education.

Oxford   New York

Auckland   Cape Town   Dar es Salaam   Hong Kong   Karachi
Kuala Lumpur   Madrid   Melbourne   Mexico City   Nairobi
New Delhi   Shanghai   Taipei   Toronto

With offices in

Argentina   Austria   Brazil   Chile   Czech Republic   France   Greece
Guatemala   Hungary   Italy   Japan   Poland   Portugal   Singapore
South Korea   Switzerland   Thailand   Turkey   Ukraine   Vietnam

Copyright © 2007 by Jim Powell

Published by Oxford University Press, Inc.
198 Madison Avenue, New York, New York 10016

www.oup.com

Oxford is a registered trademark of Oxford University Press

Library of Congress Cataloging-in-Publication Data
Sappho.
[Works. English. 2007]
The poetry of Sappho / Sappho ; translated by Jim Powell.
p. cm.
Includes bibliographical references.
ISBN 978-0-19-532671-0; 978-0-19-532672-7 (pbk.)
1. Sappho—Translations into English. 2. Love poetry,
Greek—Translations into English. I. Powell, Jim, 1951– II. Title.
PA4408.E5P69 2007
884'.01—dc22          2006101655

1 3 5 7 9 8 6 4 2

Printed in the United States of America
on acid-free paper

# CONTENTS

## ❧ Translator's Note

To facilitate reference the poems and fragments are arranged in the order of the standard edition of Lobel & Page.

Each is preceded by an ornament and followed by its number in this edition in square brackets [LP #]. Where other sources are used this is indicated. See Textual Notes for more information.

Gaps in the sequence of LP numbers indicate fragments too broken for meaningful poetic translation (see The Text of Sappho's Poems).

Square brackets in the text indicate gaps in the text where the papyrus is torn or the citation breaks off.

# THE POETRY OF SAPPHO

❦

Artfully adorned Aphrodite, deathless
child of Zeus and weaver of wiles I beg you
please don't hurt me, don't overcome my spirit,
                              goddess, with longing,

but come here, if ever at other moments
hearing these my words from afar you listened
and responded: leaving your father's house, all
                              golden, you came then,

hitching up your chariot: lovely sparrows
drew you quickly over the dark earth, whirling
on fine beating wings from the heights of heaven
                              down through the sky and

instantly arrived—and then O my blessed
goddess with a smile on your deathless face you
asked me what the matter was *this* time, what I
                              called you for this time,

what I now most wanted to happen in my
raving heart: "Whom *this* time should I persuade to
lead you back again to her love? Who *now*, oh
                              Sappho, who wrongs you?

If she flees you now, she will soon pursue you;
if she won't accept what you give, she'll give it;
if she doesn't love you, she'll love you soon now,
                    even unwilling."

Come to me again, and release me from this
want past bearing. All that my heart desires to
happen—make it happen. And stand beside me,
                    goddess, my ally.

[LP 1]


⁓

                              ] heavenly summit of the
                    mountain descending

[LP 2.1A]


⁓

Come to me from Crete to the sacred recess
of this temple: here you will find an apple
grove to welcome you and upon the altars
                    frankincense fuming.

Here ice water babbles among the apple
branches, the musk roses have overshadowed
all this ground and out of the flickering leafage
                    settles entrancement.

There are meadows, too, where the horses graze knee
deep in flowers, yes, and the breezes blow here
honey sweet and softer [
              [           ]

Here, you take a garland now also, Cypris:
gracefully in goblets of gold mix nectar
with the gladness of our festivities and
                      pour the libation.

[LP 2]

Cypris and you Néreïds, bring my brother
back to me unharmed: let him sail home safely:
grant that every one of his heart's desires
                    all be accomplished

once he makes amends for the present straying
of his ways, returning to bring great gladness
to his friends and ruin upon our enemies.
                  No longer a worry

to his sister, let him consent to do her
honor, just this once, and her cruel sorrow [

[LP 5]

### *Apropos Her Brother's Mistress*

Aphrodite, Cyprian, let her find you
at your prickliest: do not let Doríkha
crow about him coming a second time to
                              the love she is missing.

[LP 15]

Some say thronging cavalry, some say foot soldiers,
others call a fleet the most beautiful of
sights the dark earth offers, but I say it's what-
                              ever you love best.

And it's easy to make this understood by
everyone, for she who surpassed all human
kind in beauty, Helen, abandoning her
                              husband—that best of

men—went sailing off to the shores of Troy and
never spent a thought on her child or loving
parents: when the goddess seduced her wits and
                              left her to wander,

she forgot them all, she could not remember
anything but longing, and lightly straying
aside, lost her way. But that reminds me
                              now: Anactória,

she's not here, and I'd rather see her lovely
step, her sparkling glance and her face than gaze on
all the troops in Lydia in their chariots and
                    glittering armor.

[LP 16]

Close beside me now as I pray appearing,
Lady Hera, gracious in all your majesty,
you whom the Atreídai invoked to help them,
                    glorious princes,

while they were completing their many labors,
first at Ilion, and then on the ocean
sailing for this island: they hadn't power to
                    finish their journey

till they called on you, on the god of strangers
Zeus, and on Thyónë's delightful son:
now I too entreat you, O goddess, help me
                    as in the old days. [

[LP 17]

Please Abánthis, your Sappho calls you:
won't you take your Lydian lyre and play

other song to Góngyla while desire still
                           flutters your heart-strings

for that girl, that beautiful girl: her dresses'
clinging makes you shake when you see it, and I'm
happy, for the goddess herself once blamed me,
                        Our Lady of Cyprus,

for praying [

[LP 22]


∾

[                     ]

[                     ]
                ] hope of love [
                [          ]
                ] for when I look at you face to face [
then it seems to me that not even Hermíonë
matched you, and comparing you with blonde Helen's
                    nothing unseemly,

if that is permitted to mortal women.
Know this in your heart [
                  ] would free me from all my worries

[            ]
] dewy banks [
[            ]
] all night long [
[            ]

[LP 23]


❧

                    ] don't you remember [
we, too, did such things in our youth

[Voigt 24.2–4]


❧

                    ] since whomever
I do well by, they are the very ones who
                    injure me most of all.

[LP 26.2–4]


❧

Surely once you too were a delicate child:
come now, sing this, all of you, add your voices

to our celebration and grace us with your
                    company [

Yes, for we are off to a wedding: you too
know this art, so hurry and send away all
the unmarried women, and may the gods [
                    ] have [

For there is no pathway up great Olympos
                    ] for humankind [

[LP 27.4–13]


∽

maidens [
all night keeping vigil [
make a song someday of your love and of your
                    violet-lapped bride.

Come, wake up. Go summon the bachelors [
your own age so that [
we may see less sleep than the piercing-voiced [
                    nightlong nightingale.

[LP 30.2–9]

∾

In my eyes he matches the gods, that man who
sits there facing you—any man whatever—
listening from closeby to the sweetness of your
                    voice as you talk, the

sweetness of your laughter: yes, that—I swear it—
sets the heart to shaking inside my breast, since
once I look at you for a moment, I can't
                    speak any longer,

but my tongue breaks down, and then all at once a
subtle fire races inside my skin, my
eyes can't see a thing and a whirring whistle
                    thrums at my hearing,

cold sweat covers me and a trembling takes
ahold of me all over: I'm greener than the
grass is and appear to myself to be little
                    short of dying.

But all must be endured, since even a poor [

[LP 31]

∾

                    ] they have honored me with
the gift of their works

[LP 32]

Please, my goddess, goldencrowned Aphrodite,
let this lot fall to me.

[LP 33]

As the stars surrounding the lovely moon will
hide away the splendor of their appearance
when in all her fullness she shines the brightest
                                    over the whole earth

[LP 34]

whether Cyprus keeps you or Paphos or Panórmos

[LP 35]

I miss and yearn after

[LP 36]

❧

May storm winds and worries bear off the man who
    lectures my anguish

[LP 37]

❧

                 ] but intricate sandals
covered up her feet, a delightful piece of
              Lydian work.

[LP 39]

❧

   ] toward you beautiful girls my thoughts
never alter

[LP 41]

❧

When the pigeons' spirit grows cold they let their
wings droop at their sides. [

[LP 42]

] throws peace into turmoil
] weariness overcomes the heart
] settles down
] but come now, friends, dear girls,
] for day is near.

[LP 43.5–9]

## THE MARRIAGE OF HEKTOR AND ANDROMACHE

Cyprus [
The herald came [
Idaíos the swift messenger
[                              ]
"... and all the rest of Asia [    ] undying glory.
Hektor and his companions escort a dartingeyed
woman from sacred Thebë and fair Plakía's streams,
delicate Andrómache, aboard their ship
on the salt sea, and with her many golden bracelets
and scented purple robes and intricate adornments,
silver goblets past numbering and ivory."
So he said. His father leapt up eagerly

and word went to his friends throughout the spacious city.
The sons of Ilus led out mules and harnessed them
to fairwheeled carriages and all the crowd of women
and girls with slender ankles climbed on board [
and Priam's daughters separately [
And all the young unmarried men led out their stallions
and harnessed them to chariots, spirited [

                    ] charioteers [
[           *several verses missing*           ]
                    ] like the very gods
                    ] pure[
                    ]toward Ilion,
the sweetvoiced flute and kithara were mingling,
the clash of castanets, and girls' clear voices singing
a holy song. The sound rang out and reached the sky
                    ] wonderfully, lau[
Everywhere through the streets [
wine bowls and cups [
and myrrh and cassia and frankincense were mingling.
The women who were older raised a joyful cry
and all the men sang out on high, a lovely song
calling on Paian, the Farshooter, skilled with the lyre,
in praise of godlike Hektor and Andrómache.

[LP 44]

❦

] to Phoibos the Goldenhaired whom Kóeus' daughter bore
                    ] to Kronos' Son of mighty name.
But Artemis made a vow and swore the gods' great oath:
"By your head, I will remain a virgin always
    ] hunting upon the peaks of lonely mountains.
                        ] come, nod your head, grant me this favor."
So she said. The Father of the blessed gods consented,
and so the gods and people, too, call her Deershooter
    ] and also Virgin Huntress, a mighty title.
                        ] and Eros never approaches her [

[Voigt 44A]

❦

                    ] I will let my body
flow like water over the gentle cushions.

[LP 46]

❦

Then love shook my heart like the wind that falls on
                    oaks in the mountains.

[LP 47]

❧

        ] You came, and I was mad to have you:
your breath cooled my heart that was burning with desire.

[LP 48]

❧

I was in love with you, Attis, once, long ago.
To me you seemed a little girl, and not too graceful.

[LP 49]

❧

Beauty is beauty only while you gaze on it,
but the good man will presently be beautiful as well.

[LP 50]

❧

I don't know what to do. I have two thoughts.

[LP 51]

I don't expect to touch the sky.

[LP 52]

O you rosy-armed Graces, hallowed Daughters of Zeus, be here!

[LP 53]

Eros arrived from heaven wrapped in a purple mantle.

[LP 54]

### To Andrómeda

When you lie dead there will be no memory of you,
no one missing you afterward, for you have no part
in the roses of Piéria. Unnoticed in the house
of Hades, too, you'll wander, flittering after faded corpses.

[LP 55]

Not one girl, I think, will ever look on the sunlight
of another time who has such talent as this one does.

[LP 56]

### To Andrómeda

That country girl has witched your wishes,
all dressed up in her country clothes
and she hasn't got the sense
to hitch her rags above her ankles.

[LP 57]

The violet-lapped Muses' lovely gifts belong
to you now, children, and the piercing lyre, the friend of song.

My body that, before, was supple, age already
has taken by surprise, my raven tresses are turned white,

my spirit has grown heavy and my knees too weak
to carry me, that once were quick to dance as fawns.

I grumble at them often but what good is that?
For human beings to be ageless is not possible.

They say that once, for love, Dawn of the rosy arms
carried Tithonos aboard her golden bowl to the world's end

when young and handsome, but all the same in time gray age
caught up with him, although his wife was an immortal goddess.

[LP 58 new ed. West]

But delicacy, that's what I love, and this love
has made of the sun's brightness and beauty my fortune.

[LP 58.25–26]

O Dream on your dark wings
you come circling whenever sleep descends on me,

sweet god, and by your power
keep off the cruel memory of pain.

Then hope gets hold of me that I won't share
anything that the blessed gods [

for I would not be so [
these toys [

But may I have [
them all [

[Voigt 63]

"O Sappho, I love you [
the Cyprian Queen [
And yet great [
all people the sun shines on [
your glory to all lands [
and even in Ácheron you [

[LP 65.5–10]

And you, my Dika, crown your lovely locks with garlands,
twining shoots of anise in your tender hands,
for the blessed Graces come the sooner to those adorned
with flowers, and turn away from the ungarlanded.

[LP 81.6–9]

Never yet, O Írana, have I found
anyone more vexing than you.

[LP 91]

∾

[                                                            ]
"Honestly, I would like to die."
She was leaving me, saying goodbye, her cheeks

wet with tears, and she said to me:
"What a cruel unhappiness,
Sappho, I swear that I leave you against my will."

This is what I replied to her:
"Go, fare well, and remember me,
for you certainly know how we cared for you.

If you don't, why then, I would like
to remind you [
                          ] and the beautiful times we had:

for with many a crown of roses
mixed with crocus and violets
you were garlanded while you were at my side

and with many a flower necklace
you encircled your tender throat,
plaiting blossoms together to make a wreath,

and with flowery perfumes [
precious, queenly [
you anointed yourself [

and on beds of soft luxury
you would satisfy all your longing
for that tender girl [

Never was there a festival
at a shrine or a temple where
we were absent [

nor a grove or a dance [

[LP 94]

Góngyla [

surely some sign [
most of all [
Hermes entered, the guide of souls [

I said, "O my Master, [
by the blessed goddess I [
have no pleasure being above the ground:

a desire to die takes hold of me, and to see
the dewy lotus flowers
on the banks of Ácheron."

[LP 95]

] Sardis [
often turning her thoughts to this our island.

While she lived here beside us she honored you
like a goddess for all to see:
it delighted her most to hear you singing.

Now among all the women of Lydia
she stands out, just as, once the sun's
finished setting, the rosy-fingered moon

surpasses all the stars, spreading her light alike
on the salt sea and over all
the wide blossoming country meadows.

Now the dew filters down in its beauty, now
roses bloom and the tender chervil
and the flowery-scented melilot.

Often, when she goes wandering she remembers
her kind Attis, and now perhaps
her subtle heart is consumed with potent yearning.

Always her thoughts turn, longing to come where we
also think of her as her song
rises over the sea that spreads between us.

[LP 96.1–20]

∾

Though it isn't easy for us to rival
goddesses in the loveliness of their figures [

[LP 96.21–22]

∾

                              ] for my mother said

that when she was a girl if you
bound the locks of your hair in back,
gathered there in a circlet of plaited purple,

that was truly a fine adornment,
but for blondes with hair yellower
than a torch it is better to fasten it

with fresh garlands of flowers in bloom,
and more recently there were headbands
decorated in Sardis, elaborately

embroidered [

                              ] Ionian cities [

[                                                      ]
But for you, dearest Kleïs, I
have no intricate headband and
nowhere that I can get one: the Mytilénean

[                                      ]
[                                      ]
[                                      ]

these memorials of the exile
of the children of Kléanax
] horribly wasted [

[LP 98]

"Sweet mother, I can't weave my web
overcome with longing for a boy
because of slender Aphrodite."

[LP 102]

Most beautiful of all the stars
O Hesperus, bringing everything
the bright dawn scattered:
you bring the sheep, you bring the goat,
you bring the child back to her mother.

[LP 104 b & a]

❧

As a sweet apple reddens
on a high branch

at the tip of the topmost bough:
The apple-pickers missed it.

No, they didn't miss it:
They couldn't reach it.

[LP 105a]


❧

As a hyacinth in the mountains that men shepherding
tread underfoot, and to the ground its flower, all purple [

[LP 105c]


❧

As a poet of Lesbos surpasses foreigners

[LP 106]


❧

Do I really still long for virginity?

[LP 107]

O beautiful, O graceful girl

[LP 108]

We will give her, her father says.

[LP 109]

The feet of the doorkeeper
are seven fathoms long,
his sandals made of five oxhides,
ten cobblers worked to stitch them.

[LP 110]

Lift high the roofbeam,
Hymenaeus,
lift high, you carpenters:
Hymenaeus,
the groom is coming, Ares' equal,
greater far than a mortal man.

[LP 111]

Fortunate bridegroom, now the marriage that you prayed for
is accomplished, you have the girl for whom you prayed,
and *you*, bride, your appearance is full of grace, your eyes
are gentle and love wells on your delightful face:
Aphrodite has honored you beyond all others.

[LP 112]

For you, O bridegroom, there was never another girl like this one.

[LP 113]

"Virginity, virginity, where have you gone and left me?"
"Never again will I come to you, never again."

[LP 114]

To what shall I best liken you, dear bridegroom?
Most of all to a slender sapling I liken you.

[LP 115]

Farewell, O bride, farewell O honored groom, farewell

[LP 116]

Come now, my holy lyre,
find your voice and speak to me.

[Voigt 118]

But I'm not one of those with a resentful
temperament: I have a quiet heart.

[LP 120]

And since you are my friend
get yourself a younger bedmate
for I can't bear to keep house together
being the elder.

[LP 121]

❧

a tender girl picking flowers

[LP 122]

❧

Just now Dawn in her golden sandals [

[LP 123]

❧

In my season I used to weave love garlands.

[LP 125]

❧

May you sleep upon your gentle companion's breast.

[LP 126]

❧

Come to me once more, O you Muses, leaving
golden [

[LP 127]

❧

Come to me now, you delicate Graces and you fairtressed Muses

[LP 128]


❧

You have forgotten me
or else you love another more than me.

[LP 129]


❧

Eros limbslackener shakes me again—
that sweet, bitter, impossible creature.

[LP 130]


❧

But Attis, to you the thought of me grows
hateful, and you fly off to Andrómeda.

[LP 131]

I have a beautiful little girl: the golden flowers
are no match for her loveliness, my darling Kleïs
—for her, I wouldn't take all Lydia or sweet [

[LP 132]

Sappho, why do you summon Aphrodite
rich in blessings? [

Andrómeda certainly has her fair return.

[LP 133 a & b]

Goddess, I spoke with you in a dream,
Cyprus-born Aphrodite

[LP 134]

Why, O Írana, does Pandíon's daughter the swallow
wake me?

[LP 135]

❧

spring's messenger, the lovelyvoiced nightingale

[LP 136]

❧

### In Answer To Alcaeus

[       ]
"I want to tell you something, and yet my shame
          prevents me ..." [
                              [                                    ]

But if you wanted good things or lovely ones
and if your tongue weren't stirring up something bad
          to say then shame would never hide your
                    eyes: you would state your case [

[LP 137]

❧

But stand before me, if you are my friend,
and spread the grace that's in your eyes.

[LP 138]

He is dying, Cytheréa, Adonis the delicate. What shall we do?
"Beat your breasts, girls, and tear your clothes."

[LP 140]

There a bowl of ambrosia
was mixed and ready
and Hermes took the pitcher and poured wine for the gods.
They all held glasses
and made libations, praying all good things
for the groom.

[LP 141]

Now Leto and Níobë were very dear companions

[LP 142]

golden chickpeas grew along the shore

[LP 143]

❦

certainly now they've had quite enough
of Gorgo.

[LP 144]

❦

For me
neither the honey
nor the bee.

[LP 146]

❦

I think that someone will remember us in another time.

[LP 147]

❦

Wealth without virtue is no harmless neighbor.

[LP 148]

when nightlong slumber closes their eyes

[LP 149]

In the house of the Muses' servants
grief is not right. It would not suit us.

[LP 150]

over the eyes night's black slumber

[LP 151]

mingled with colors of every kind

[LP 152]

a sweetvoiced girl

[LP 153]

The moon appeared in all her fullness
and so the women stood around the altar.

[LP 154]

Let me wish the child of the house of Polyanax a
very good day.

[LP 155]

far more melodious than the lyre,
more golden than gold

[LP 156]

Mistress Dawn

[LP 157]

When anger spreads inside your breast
keep watch against an idly barking tongue.

[LP 158]

And Aphrodite said
"Sappho, you and my attendant Eros" [

[LP 159]

Now to delight my women friends
I'll make a beautiful song of this affair.

[LP 160]

*with what eyes?*

[LP 162]

❧

For they say that Leda once found a hyacinth
colored egg, all covered [

[LP 166]

❧

Moonset already,
the Pleiades, too: midnight,
the hour passes
and I lie down, a lonely woman.

[Voigt 168B]

❧

Earth with her many garlands
is embroidered

[Voigt 168C]

❧

Eros, weaver of tales

[LP 188]

Fool, don't try to bend a stubborn heart.

[Incertum 5.3]

Delicate girl, in the old days
I strayed from you, and now again [

[Incertum 5.4]

Cretan women once danced this way
on gentle feet in time
around the lovely altar, softly
treading the tender flowers of grass.

[Incertum 16 a & b]

Hékate, the shining gold attendant of Aphrodite

[Incertum 23]

Like a child to her mother I have flown to you.

[Incertum 25]

These are Timas's ashes: on the threshold of her marriage
she died and entered Persephone's dark house instead,
and all the girls who were her friends took fresh-honed iron
to the long locks of their lovely hair and laid them on this grave.

[EG, Sappho II]

## ⌣ Sappho of Lesbos

Sappho's poetry made her famous throughout the ancient Greek world, probably within her lifetime. Soon, like the medieval French poet François Villon, she became a subject of legend and figured later as a character in comedy. Surviving biographical facts are few and are transmitted to us mixed up with the lore of fables and with bits of dramatic fiction.[*] Sappho was born on Lesbos around 630 b.c., probably in the town of Eresos, but spent most of her life in Mytilene, the most important of the island's five cities. Her mother's name was Kleïs; her father's name may have been Skamandronymos. She was orphaned at the age of six. Her family was socially prominent and politically active.

Lesbos was settled by Aeolic Greeks in the eleventh century b.c. In Sappho's time, five generations after Homer, it had a flourishing economic, religious, and artistic culture, connections throughout the eastern Mediterranean, and a vibrant local poetic tradition of long-standing and wide fame. The eldest of Sappho's three brothers, Charáxos, was a merchant captain trading in Egypt; there, to his sister's displeasure, he became involved with an Egyptian courtesan whom Sappho calls Doríkha (see LP 5 and 15; her real name may have been Rhodópis). Another brother, Lárichos, poured the wine for the

---

[*] Campbell conveniently collects the surviving ancient biographical testimony. See Abbreviations and Bibliography for complete references.

Mytileneans at their town hall, a public "office reserved," C. M. Bowra writes, "for young men of good birth and handsome appearance." Sappho must have been married young; she had a daughter named Kleïs (LP 98 and 132), and they lived in exile in Sicily during her thirties (LP 98), presumably as a result of her family's political activities, but later returned to Lesbos, where her tomb was pointed out to tourists in antiquity. She probably died after 570 b.c. She is reputed to have been short, dark, and ugly.

## ∾ THE TEXT OF SAPPHO'S POEMS

We do not know how Sappho put her poems into circulation. Echoes of her phrases in Pindar, Aeschylus, and others show that her poetry was widely recognized and admired. Ten generations after her death two of the great scholars of Alexandria in the third and second centuries b.c., Aristophanes of Byzantium and Aristarchus of Samothrace, collected and edited her poems in nine books arranged according to meter. The first book (scroll, that is), assembling poems in her eponymous sapphic stanza (e.g., LP 1), contained 1,320 verses; others were probably shorter, but still it is apparent that originally the corpus of her poetry was fairly substantial. By way of comparison this translation, comprising all the surviving fragments of her work that make consecutive sense, however brief, torn, or abruptly interrupted, contains around 500 verses.

For another dozen generations Sappho's poetry continued to attract the attention and praise of listeners, readers, poets, and scholars, and in the first century b.c. it exercised a seminal influence on the flowering of Latin lyric in the poetry of Catullus and on the *Odes* of Horace. But by the period of late antiquity (fifth–seventh centuries a.d.), when it became imperative for ancient literary texts to be transcribed from scrolls to books in sufficient numbers if they were to have a chance of surviving the ensuing epoch of social upheaval and cultural collapse, the contracting literary interests of the culture and the "obscurity" of Sappho's Aeolic dialect in a world where Attic Greek had triumphed combined to bring about the eventual loss of her collected poetry. There is evidence suggesting that Byzantine scholars in the tenth and eleventh centuries had access to works of Sappho now lost, but if so, these texts must have perished in the flames when the Fourth Crusade sacked Constantinople in 1204.

From the renaissance of the knowledge of ancient Greek in Europe until the 1890s the only texts of Sappho available to readers were one complete poem, saved because quoted by the critic Dionysius of Halicarnassus (LP 1), the first 17 verses of another preserved in Longinus's *On The Sublime* (LP 31), and around 100 brief fragments, usually no more than a word or a phrase, quoted by various ancient grammarians, lexicographers, philosophers, scholars, and rhetoricians whose works' survival had been sponsored by the interest of medieval schoolmasters.

Since the 1890s, however, our access to Sappho's poetry has been greatly increased by the discovery of around 100 more fragments on papyrus (one on a potsherd) unearthed by archaeologists mostly in Egypt during the first decades of the twentieth century and gradually deciphered, edited, and published. All of them are mutilated in some degree, many far too seriously to allow them to yield consecutive poetic sense—LP 67, for instance, a scrap of a strip of papyrus torn from the middle of a column of verse to mummify a crocodile:

> ]nd this overhan[
> ]tructive spirit[
> ]truly did not lik[
> ] and now because [
> ] the cause neither [
> ]nothingmuch[

Not all papyri of Sappho are as pathetically mutilated as this one, and several number among her most important surviving texts (e.g., LP 16, 44, 94, and 96). In 1955 Edgar Lobel and Denys Page assembled and published these new papyrus texts together with the already extant fragments in *Poetarum Lesbiorum Fragmenta*, the standard modern edition of Sappho's poetry in the original Aeolic Greek (LP; it also contains the surviving fragments of the poetry of her compatriot and contemporary, Alcaeus).

In recent years advances in photographic imaging techniques and the use of computers to facilitate and speed the reassembly of fragments have begun to assist with the decipherment of papyri. Texts previously illegible can now sometimes be read and the puzzle pieces of the fragments are more easily and rapidly assembled. A fresh surge of progress in papyrology may be beginning. Already in 2004 there appeared a newly discovered complete text of LP 58, known previously only as a brief, badly tattered fragment. It is amazing and delightful, 2,600 years after her birth and at least 800 since it was last read, to witness another complete poem of Sappho emerging into the light of day anew. Happily, there is a plausible prospect of more new recoveries.

## ∿ ABBREVIATIONS AND BIBLIOGRAPHY

Bowra, Cecil Maurice, *Greek Lyric Poetry*, Oxford, Oxford University Press, 2nd rev. ed., 1961.

Campbell = David A Campbell, ed. and trans., *Greek Lyric*, Cambridge, Mass., Harvard University Press (Loeb Library Series), vol. 1, *Sappho and Alcaeus*, 1982.

Edmonds = Edmonds, J. M., ed. and trans., *Lyra Graeca*, London, William Heinemann, 2nd pr. 1928, vol. 1 (superseded Loeb Library edition).

EG = *Epigrammata Graeca*, ed. Denys Page, Oxford, Oxford University Press, 1975.

Incertum = LP, Incertum Utrius Auctoris Fragmenta, i.e., fragments which LP is unsure whether to assign to Sappho or Alcaeus, and here assigned to Sappho.

LP = Edgar Lobel and Denys Page, eds., *Poetarum Lesbiorum Fragmenta*, Oxford, Oxford University Press, 1955.

Page = Denys Page, *Sappho and Alcaeus*, Oxford, Oxford University Press, rpr. with corr., 1959 (an edition and commentary on twelve major texts of Sappho).

PMG = *Poetae Melici Graeci*, ed. Denys Page, Oxford, Oxford University Press, rpr. with corr. 1967.

Voigt = Eva-Maria Voigt, ed., *Sappho et Alcaeus: Fragmenta*, Amsterdam, Athenaeum, 1971.

West = Martin L. West, "A New Sappho Poem" (*Times Literary Supplement* No. 5334, June 24, 2005, p. 8).

## ∾ TEXTUAL NOTES

To prepare these translations in cases where the text is in question I consulted three, four, or more editions of Sappho's Greek—principally LP (1955, still the "standard edition"), Page (1959), Campbell (1982), and Voigt (1971). The readings of the first three tend cumulatively to reinforce each other; Voigt offers an independent view of the text as well as a copious Apparatus Criticus.

The basic text translated is indicated following each poem or fragment. Below I note only where the translated text differs from the standard edition (LP). Usually this is a matter of readings or supplements adopted by Page and/or Campbell, often from the apparatus criticus of LP. On a few occasions I adopt readings from Voigt's apparatus, or from Campbell's, or from Page's commentary.

LP 1: This translation accepts the argument advanced by Michael Putnam that the second component of the first epithet Sappho applies to Aphrodite, -*thron'*, is to be derived not from *thronos* ("throne") but from *throna* (a "love charm" attached to dress, perhaps embroidered); see "*Throna* and Sappho 1.1" (*Classical Journal* 56.2, 1960, 79–83). Readers who prefer may substitute for "adorned" "enthroned."

LP 2.1a: According to one reading of the textual evidence this is the conclusion of a stanza preceding the next (LP 2.1 ff.); according to the other LP 2.1 is the beginning of a new poem and this is part of another.

LP 2, with Diehl's reading in 3–4 and Page's in 8.

LP 5, as supplemented in Campbell.

LP 16.1–20, with Campbell's reading in 19, LP's conjecture in 8, and Rackham's in 20. 12–16 represent my reconstruction of Sappho's sense from the seven words of the passage still legible; I regard 21 ff. as the beginning of a new poem.

LP 17, as supplemented in Page.

LP 22.9–17, with 9–10 as supplemented in Campbell.

LP 23, with Castiglioni's conjecture in 3, Page's in 4–6, Wilamowitz's in 7, Diehl's in 8, and Hunt's in 13.

LP 27.4–13, with Voigt's reading in 7, Treu's conjectures in 4, Snell's in 8, mine in 9 (tachista [*paisais*]), and Theander's in 12.

LP 30.2–9, with Lobel's supplements in 6–8.

LP 31, with Voigt's reading and Sitzler's conjecture in 9, Page's reading in 13, and reading with Voigt 213B.8 in 16.

LP 34, with Holt Okes and Ahrens's conjecture in 4.

LP 44 is a poem in which Sappho adopts the "old fashioned" language and style of Aeolic heroic narrative, a tradition related to Homer's.

Voigt 44A = LP 304, "Alcaeus T 1."

LP 50, with Hermann's conjecture in 1.

LP 55, with Bucherer's reading in 2.

LP 58 new ed. West: I translate the Greek text as supplemented by Martin L. West, "A New Sappho Poem" (*Times Literary Supplement*

No. 5334, June 24, 2005, p. 8) but in the tenth verse prefer the reading of the first publication, by Michael Gronewald and Robert Daniels in *Zeitschrift für Papyrologie und Epigraphik* #149 (2004) 1 ff.

LP 58.25–26: The new papyrus that gives us LP 58 nearly complete shows that these verses belong to a different poem.

Voigt 63, with Hunt's conjecture in 1, Latte's in 2, and Diehl's in 3 and 4.

LP 94: In 22 "girl" is derived from the suggestion of the gender of the adjective *apalan* ("tender").

LP 95, with Blass' conjecture in 11.

LP 96.1–20, with Kamerbeek's reading in 17. 18–20 represent my reconstruction of Sappho's sense from the eight words of this stanza still legible. I regard 21 ff. ("Though it isn't easy") as the beginning of a new poem.

LP 135, as supplemented in Campbell.

LP 148.1; 148.2 is the palliative amendment of an interpolator.

LP 160, with Sitzler's conjecture.

Voigt 168B = PMG 976.

Incert. 5.3, as in Edmonds 93.
Incert. 5.4, as supplemented in Edmonds 96.
EG, Sappho II = *Greek Anthology* 7.489.